Wendy Fren

Bread without Butter

Bara heb fenyn

Angela

with love + friendship

Wendy

July 2020

Rockingham Press

We'll keep going! x

Published in 2020 by
Rockingham Press
11 Musley Lane,
Ware, Herts SG12 7EN
www.rockinghampress.co.uk

British Library Cataloguing-in-Publication Data

A catalogue record for this book
is available from the British Library

ISBN   978-1-904851-81-3

The poems in this book are dedicated to
Isabella, Alexia and Kiya.
The poems are about their ancestry.

I also remember my step-grandchildren, who are not Welsh,
but are part of our history now:
Alexander, Nicholas, William, Edward, Evie and Roman.

Acknowledgements

I am grateful to the editors of the following magazines and journals where some of these poems, or versions of them, appeared: Acumen, Artemis, Avalanche Books, London-Grip, And Other Poems, Intima Journal, Seren pamphlet series on Pembrokeshire, Magma, Poems and Pictures, Poetry Space, Born in the NHS, co-written with Jane Kirwan, Hippocrates press.

I am indebted to friends and poets (particularly our Wednesday night group led by Jane Duran). I also attended a group led by Kathryn Maris where I met more good friends and poets. I should also mention the monthly Sunday group who give on-going support. In particular I would like to mention the following people who, over the years, have cajoled me into thinking again: Jane Duran (again) Mimi Khalvati, Anne-Marie Fyfe, Les Robinson, Chris Beckett, Danielle Hope, Lynne Hjelmgaard, Jane Kirwan, Rebecca Goss, Robert Seatter, Audrey Ardern-Jones, Maggie Sawkins.

Henry Thomas, my cousin, grew up on Bwlchydomen Farm and supplied me with snippets of information I had forgotten or not known about.

And as ever, thanks to David Perman of Rockingham Press, who in spite of all the difficulties of this year, has helped me to pursue this project.

Preface

Tom came home, fortuitously, in March from working in China/ Vietnam with a reproduction of a picture by Gauguin. The painting is called: *Where do we come from? What are we? Where are we going?* The title of the picture fitted in with my work.

So why call the book *Bread without Butter*? It is not meant to signify deprivation but a connection between people and the earth, the very basics of life, not the icing but the bare facts of our own individual existence with its trials and triumphs.

The poems I have been writing are connected to family, past and present. Ours is not a nuclear family as marriage, divorce, stepchildren, grandchildren, sisters and their children, cousins, all interwoven increase the notion of family and belonging.

This immediately made me think about the poems in this collection, made up as it is of poems about my past, our ancestors, the present. The Covid 19 virus took hold of our lives as this work was being drawn to a conclusion so I've added two very new poems. It is the effect of 'lockdown' on ordinary peoples' lives that I am concerned about.

These poems are all about ordinary people, us. Life is very different in rural Wales now from when our grandparents lived. Their hardships lessened with the advance in science and technology but other hardships took over. The strong sense of community has gone. Children and siblings moved away and strangers moved in.

Wendy French

Contents

Hiraeth

Mamgu's voice comes through the night
Stop harrowing me bach   let me rest

No Mamgu you're harrowing me
like the farmers ploughed the fields
with their old ploughs, you harrow me
you're frying bacon on the range
watching the clock for 8 am
for the men who come in from the fields

Mamgu grandmother

Farmer's daughter

Travelling back from overseas
with his knapsack and worn boots
over lands he thought he knew,

down lanes until he could see
milk-churns waiting for collection,
through lanes he thought he'd forgotten

but she'd gone, they told him gone away,
married a doctor. All he could see
were men he'd left injured, left them

dying for this – he remembered
the stuffed badger in her bedroom
her red ink on school books

and the meeting he had rehearsed sunk
like promises he'd made.
He ate tea with the farmer's wife

in the kitchen he knew so well – she was there,
the farmer's daughter, pouring tea for her father,
her deft hands breaking scones.

The doctor's wife
1943

Up the Ton Mawr Road, uncharted night,
where snow has buried the trees,
the moon lights up the old car
that can't climb any further.

Ice devours everything, even a couple
walking against night. The sheep are bleating
ignored by the shepherd who listens for a knock,
boils kettles, piles up the towels.

Two figures struggle on to the croft
on this night where the air consumes even
the most human of souls. The doctor's wife
knows what she has to do, make the tea,

hold the woman, time the contractions.
Doctor and shepherd wait for a whisky.
She wonders about love on a night like this.
The screams, the cries, the joy, the pain and ice.

Fields

My mother, failing fast, mutters
in a language she'd never permit us
to learn, certain it would hold us back –

her *diolch* and *bore da* and *bara heb fenyn*
three whispered phrases we might speak
or eat, *bara heb fenyn*, staff of all life,

bread without butter,
one-eyed fishes thrown to the crowd.
We hold our tongues, her breath fills

the river's river, flows at the boundary
by the field we were never allowed to cross,
the horizon beyond vision.

She stares towards the east where altars are laid,
the dead rise or so we believe and doubt.
My mother more Welsh than yesterday. Her eye

is failing her ear, her ear is failing. What cloud
fills her eye, what absence of breath this Wednesday.
She lies on her back, hovers between fields.

diolch   thank you
bore da   good morning
bara heb fenyn   bread without butter

Migration

My mother is dying and you're recounting names
of forty-seven species of birds you've seen
this weekend. Your purpose is to look up,
identify and record their habits.

She's mumbling in sleep, words she's trying to find.
You're writing down in your notebook
spoonbill, linnet, siskin, white-fronted goose,
barnacle goose, pintail.

My mother is dying as you tell me about the man
who took so long fumbling with his telescope
the black-tailed godwit gave up, flew South.
Redshank, mute swan are the birds you'll write

to Ales about, the migratory siskin is a name
that stays with me.

Stories I heard while drying my hair

Fifty years on, my mother longs for sheared wool,
aches to caress it. In winter months she is her mother.
Wears a coarse woollen cap.

She looks in the mirror and sees the farmhouse,
sees Mamgu rise, sees her rub frost
from inside the window pane.

Stories in front of the stove in the stone kitchen.
Chickens scratch around in the yard.
In the night I rehearse the line,

my favourite, about the harvest moon,
how it fades in the sky and the other
that begins with a silence, a girl and the cry

of a bird. My mother's distant voice
in the pull of my hairbrush.

Gone shopping

My mother calls at least five times a day.
The times are noted daily in her book:

When I'm not in she leaves a message,
I can't find your Dad

and ends, *Oh, Mum here.*
As if I wouldn't recognise this frail accent

coming down the line or through the air.
When my sister was there at an appointed time

she tried to phone me using the remote control.
Once she phoned me at 3 pm and I was sitting there.

To the answerphone she said, *I can't find Dad.*
To me she said, *She's not in.*

'Perhaps she's gone shopping,' I replied.
Oh no! She'll be out looking for her Dad.

And I am, Mum. Five times a day. I'm out now,
searching everywhere for both of you.

Somewhere

God and rain have deserted the hills.
The rooster calls from the yard so it has to be Sunday.

Once my father sang along to Forces' Request,
something about a girl in the world.

Elsewhere the rain, bells and on this sort of day,
in a story I read, a spy once walked to Tower Bridge.

My mother calls. Her flowers are wilting,
Charlie hasn't been for weeks

and it's a year since your father died.
The red tapestry table cloth is now rags.

9 a.m. chimes so Lucille will be leaving home,
turban woven tightly round her head.

She'll nurse her cancer, holding her arm
as she takes her singing to the gospel choir.

And my mother is trying to tell me something

in a voice I don't understand and I'm listening hard,
worrying she'll think I'm a teenager again,
flaunting in front of her and refusing to listen
and *Mama* I say *I am listening but I'm not sure
what you want* and I revert to her old name *Mama*,
offering my hair for a brush and a braid, it will hurt,
it always does. A carer comes in to paint her nails
and I say *No!*
        And the carer says *she always liked
to look smart* and I say *but she's past that now*
and the carer says *how would you know?* I'm angry,
not wanting to hear a stranger knows my mother
better than I do, my mother whispers, *rwy'n ar goll*
I lean in, she pats my hand, takes a chunk of my hair,
ready for me to lead her on.

rwy'n ar goll   I'm lost

Bwlchydomen farm, our farm

a kitchen   like no other   the hum and hisstle
yes that word   will do of a range that lives on
like the oldest of the apple trees
                    in the orchard

hams hang from a beam   held by gigantic screws
a brown teapot   never empty   and boots
boots caked in mud
                    by the scullery door

jams   marmalades   pickles stored for winter
milk bottles   butter pats   on slabs   and Mamgu
on her knees   scrubbing the floor   a small farmhouse
                    in a corner of Wales

cows are milked   lambs born   men fed   an old woman dies
a child is born a young girl suffering with tonsillitis
has her tonsils removed   as she lies
                    on the kitchen table

You are Welsh, they said;
Speak to us so...

R.S. Thomas 'A Welsh Testament'

Gambling is a sin, Mamgu says

Mamgu deals the cards, drinks
Dutch gin by the tumblerful
and wins every time.

The room is lit by two candles,
one lightbulb and the old coal fire
that takes the whole evening to warm

the room before we go to bed.
She's given up on prayers,
nothing can save her now.

I've seen it all: nothing can surprise me now

If God had been a woman, conception and birth
would have been easier, Mamgu thinks
as she trudges to Pwll-Trap in blizzards
to help Alwyn in labour
her thoughts hardened against night

and *Johnny bach* trudging over other fields
to find the doctor runs, half walks, half cries
against the wet, Tadcu in the cowshed
a cow in difficulty and the vet, his van stuck,
striding on the Llangynin Road

and then there'd been the heatwave
Max the spaniel drowned looking for water
Natte the trapper unable to sell mangy fox
for a penny, farmers want the bright red skin
of winter to barter for a shilling

Dai the water diviner couldn't find water
and the grass was parched
water preserved from one bath for four people
Mamgu's tomatoes must be saved
and little Myfanwy in a fever

and then Elizabeth comes down
and tells her that Philip   the dentist's son
is the father of Eliza's baby not Tom and Tom
hits Philip so hard on the Sancler road
he falls in to the ditch and stays there 'til morning

Tadcu grandfather

God is Welsh

On Sundays Welsh flowed over our heads.
We longed for the park
with the no-good boys of summer.

Now my mother mumbles and
caught between *tatws* and turnips
she rolls and turns in her bed.

Mamgu knew God was Welsh.
I don't need to worship, your mam goes for me.
London's a place where prayer's needed.

Mae Iesu'n newidiamar dwr i win.
This was the one miracle Mamgu told us
not to listen to, perhaps thinking of her preference

for Dutch gin. Nibby, the boy, next door,
came to *capel* once, then borrowed my toy boat
to sail on West Harrow pond.

tatws (pronounced tatters): potatoes
Mae Iesus'n newidiamar dwr i win: Jesus changes water to wine.
capel: chapel

Mamgu and Tadcu

In Mamgu's stories seconds become minutes
with her immaculate timing as she entertains us,
her peculiar grandchildren from London.

We count predictable ten seconds before the punchline
and although we could have told the stories for her
we wait for a terrifying delivery.

Capel going had taught her all she knows.
We do not speak her language but we know
when excited she never forgets a word.

Our favourite is about the deaf and dumb man,
(Mamgu calls him) who stabbed his mother
for lack of a bacon sandwich.

She tells this story as she's frying bacon for the men
coming in from the fields. *Nothing is worth dying for*
and then she adds, *Gambling and lying are sins.*

*   *   *

Mamgu takes my face in her two hands
squeezes tightly, looks straight into my eyes,
Are you telling the truth? Are you telling lies?

And I am not telling the truth.
I want to protect John-Jack from Pwll-Trap
who grew up as a lie knowing his father

had disappeared and rumour went round
the farm-kids he'd been found under a cow
before milking one morning.

*   *   *

After the caving in of the Rhondda mine's walls,
Mamgu gave up going to *capel* on Sundays.
It was wrong that her brother, an inspector

of ponies, should die this way. *My faith's my own.*
I'll find it in the parsley.
She'd be all night in the lambing shed

and cook breakfast for the men in from milking.
With time she relented and went to *capel*
for weddings and funerals.

She was worried about being the only person at hers.
Her faith was private until age wore her down.
She made us promise when she lay in the coffin

we'd place some sheep's wool in her fist
so God would know she'd been a shepherd
and couldn't worship Him on Sundays.

*   *   *

And when the harvest failed or a calf was still-born
Mamgu would pack a picnic, and send us
to Pendine for the day whatever the tide,

even at the height of summer – a thermos of scalding
hot tomato soup, home-made sausage rolls,
thick bread with churned butter.

She said if the waves were too far in
we could sit on the cliffs. Tadcu would drive us
in his old Austin, once it started.

We'd be delighted with sandcastles, moats,
scratching words in the sand with sticks.
We'd try to guess each other's words

before they disappeared. Tadcu wrote in Welsh.
We'd have to guess, he'd laugh. Tiny hermit crabs
crawled deep into the sand.

* * *

Mamgu embraced the land.
Snow or scorching sun she'd wear her blanket
over shoulders, stride out to look at her *tatws*

still buried in the earth, deep as seedlings,
or showing shoots in the spring.
She'd dig her potatoes with arthritic hands,

fill buckets and the air with the words
of her favourite song, *Calon lan,*
She said she was the land, *It is me now.*

*   *   *

Mamgu pinned a map on her wall, marked
with a pin places where friends and family visited.
The doctor's wife was keen on statues and ruins.

She sent a card from the Colosseum.
Mamgu wondered why travel so far to see ruins.
There's ruins on the Llangynin Road why go further?

What's romantic about a body with no eyes?
You can't know what he's thinking.
She'd love to go to St Fagan's to see the creation.

The only creation for Tadcu brought money.
Look at that bull in amongst the herd of cows.
She loved the way waves hit the shore, beauty

in a sheaf of corn, a red berry on a holly bush
and the seasons changing.
Sometimes, she said, *Tadcu has no soul.*

*   *   *

When other Mamgus came down to the farm
animated with news they didn't want us to hear
they spoke in Welsh. We could tell by their faces

talk that shocked them but made them alive again –
carried them away from the fields and scrubbing floors –
to make the news their own.

Each of them wanting to be the young girl carried
to the woods by the intruder farmer from another town.
It was the way they would stand tall, pull in their stately waists

and sigh. We knew how they thrived on these tales,
grew bright with longing and we'd giggle later
about Auntie King's Park who swooned once.

The smelling salts found she soon came round
and we guessed that once back on her own farm
she'd lie awake most of the night hating Great-Uncle Tom

who lay beside her, snoring, wishing she could have her time again
and afraid, now, to look at her friends' faces
but more worried about going to *capel* on Sunday.

                    *   *   *

Mamgu had never had a holiday. Said she'd love to go to
The Metropole in Llandrindnod Wells, she'd read about
in The Western Mail. Llandrindod Wells is fifty miles from

the farm. Tadcu said *No*, she wouldn't know what to do in a hotel where
her bed would be made every day by a maid and she wouldn't be allowed
in the kitchen to supervise the cooking of bacon

and what would she do after breakfast?
She'd sit in the lounge observing the other guests in their finery, wearing
her black skirt, white blouse and cameo brooch fastened

at her neck. And what would they do? How would he know which knife and fork to use at supper? Tadcu had seen pictures in magazines of stately homes and banquets.

Anyway, he liked plain food and who'd look after the cows?
And what would he do while she talked with other mamgus?
She pondered this and said that perhaps she could go on her own.

Tadcu said it would be an absolute waste of money and anyway she was needed here to feed the men not swan around a spa town getting ideas.

They came to the farm looking for work

Slept in the barns, sacking and hay for bedding.
Mamgu fed them up three meals a day,
Tadcu gave a few shillings for a couple o' pints.
We became friends, no one spoke the same language.
Michael was our favourite – no tooth in his head,
trousers held up with a piece of string.
He understood the cows as if he was one of them.
Michael did magic in the barns, made coins disappear.
He gurgled milk straight from a cow, day after day.

He laughed at our English, *ugh*!
We gave him the response he craved.
Mamgu poured him a pint of tea every meal
to dip bread in, he couldn't chew. Mamgu felt sorry
for him. *Even the cows can chew cud.*
One night he moved on. Did night skies remind him
of a gap in his life? This giant, sweaty man with no home.
Cows took longer to reach the parlour without his calls,
a kind of *gerrrup* as he struck his legs with his cap.

Old Tom

Yes, there was old Tom, faithful as a sheepdog, he'd never been married. Some say it was because he couldn't keep tuppence in his pocket, money burnt a hole in all his hand-me-down clothes, He slept in the hayloft, climbed the outside ladder to bed every night except Saturdays, pay day, when he was too inebriated to walk from The Black Lion. We never knew where he slept on Saturdays. He was the first one up every morning to bring in the cows and his defining walk echoed over the farmyard. He always wore the same tweed jacket, one of my father's cast-offs, and a flat cap he told us he slept in to keep his brains warm. His brains were needed in the fields not for reading and writing. He never bathed as far as we knew but he was the strongest man we knew, skeletal, even though Mamgu fed him well. He swam in the river in the summer and he laughed out loud when we asked him if he owned a costume. If there was a cow in trouble he was the first to rescue her (until Michael came for they worked day and night together). Once Alywn, a young heifer, slipped down the slagging mud and we watched as he stood in icy water to comfort her until Michael came to help haul her out. The youngest of nine he never talked about family, *Cows that's all I need, and a pint now and again* as he grinned.

Old Tom taught us to respect even the tiniest daisy in a field of hundreds. After Michael left, he never mentioned him. Carried on working as if he'd always been alone.

Bluebell Wood

two men   boys actually
scrub down the milking parlour
leave it smelling sweet
they've learnt not to ask questions
can you see how they run to the bluebell wood
breaking cobwebs with breath as they go
fight each other   roll on the ground
one clutches his stomach
the other urinates over his hard-worn boots
how they laugh   laugh
before they trudge back to the farmhouse

Billy

Billy worked on the farm, only sixteen, left school at twelve to help his mother raise siblings. One of his tasks was to collect the newspaper from San Cler. A four-mile walk, country lanes, there and back. Once he took a short cut. Skated on thin ice. Promised never to do that again. Mamgu told us that Tadcu had asked, *How would your mother manage without you?* And then she found him dry clothes. Dried the Western Mail on the range. One Monday he turned up with two papers. *Why two? Save me going tomorrow* he said.

The day Billy's conscription papers arrived he was just eighteen, proud to be called to fight. He waited impatiently for orders to go and collect his uniform and kitbag, rushed back to the farm to show off his clothes and found he had the best made trousers he'd ever had in his life. He thought a billy-can was a hat. Stuck it on his head and marched round the stone floor kitchen. Saluting. A week later he left the farm for training. His mother was seen standing outside Eynons the butchers, on the High Street. Hands tightly clasped.

Chicken run

The farm boy chased me round the farm with a half-plucked, half-feathered chicken. It was on its way to the oven for supper. The squawks of the hens, still alive, frightened me more than the chase. Chicken was on the menu weekly. I fell in cow dung and he flung the bird at me, it was twitching, I lay in the dung petrified. My father explained it was due to the nervous system. The creature was dead. This haunted me at night. I imagined the dead birds coming back although they'd already filled our plates. It was my fault there'd been the chase and the hen flung in the air after death, not buried in the grave that I'd dug for my doll when I'd smashed its face. Or indeed not thrown in the hole my father had dug for my grandfather's ashes. The birds would come back. They haunted me night after night. If spirits return from the grave, do birds come back half-plucked, half-feathered?

On the road to Haverfordwest

Once an hour another old Mamgu opens her front door,
peers and waves in the hope someone will pass,
stop, spend a few coppers on a bag of fresh manure.

She's alone, has enough coal for a few days but
nothing keeps her warm. A van pulls up
and for a rare moment she is happy.

A child clambers out, pulls down his trousers
by the grass verge and pees in the snow,
leaves a yellow trail.

Mamgu's room

With age she retreated to the back room
which overlooked ducks swimming on the pond.
The room contained little, her dressing table,

made skilfully by Great Uncle Tom,
had two small drawers with handkerchiefs
and a cameo brooch worn on Sundays.

A lace cloth covered the table-top, a silver hairbrush
she was proud to own and a jar of Pond's cold cream.
God bless our home hung from a small mirror.

Mamgu said she didn't need a bigger one,
she knew what she looked like and anyway
there was no time to look at herself in the day.

Did she see more than a grey-haired woman
with eyes tired and secrets engrained in her?
Rumours had it her mother was a tyrant.

No photographs remain of those days
I want to know who this other Welsh woman was.
Who am I? Stockings hung over iron bed posts

and a wardrobe housed few clothes.
The bedside table held her mother's bible,
one clock and glass of water.

*   *   *

Once she'd lived, balanced between fields.
Conscription papers for all young farmers.
The willow pattern plates still balance

on the Welsh dresser and catch sunlight
from cornfields. Cows still drink at the trough,
altars and cowsheds face the east

where rivers ran dry in war-time.
Fields were parched with decaying wheat
and she remembers a young girl waiting

at the top of the lane for news of her brother.
Cows, lambs registered with the war office,
take their turn at the grass.

She dusts the cracked plate she'd broken
on purpose and she laughs at how beautiful
she was then but remembers each day hurt.

*   *   *

Mamgu never draws the curtains
instead draws strength from the timelessness
of feeling neither young nor old.

Bwlchydomen Farm 1959

Christmas Eve

light enters through the stained glass
        of a kitchen window
                lands on the dish of tangerines

moonlight enters a bathroom
        through a skylight
                lands on the washstand covered in holly

light from the matches struck by the farm-hand
        as he winds his snow-way home
                thoughts of mistletoe and his favourite girl

light from an old torch as the farmer delivers a calf
        in the frost-lit hours of Christmas morning
                and gives thanks for its birth

six candles light up the front door
        to mark Mamgu's dying —
                we slide back the bolt to let her spirit
breathe

One blade of grass

Come and I come – Paddington Station to San Cler
my grandfather's horse and cart to meet me
in the station forecourt, only it isn't there

because the horse is now dead and the cart
was firewood, long ago.
Heavy shoes clump on this earth and I wait

for my cousin who drives furiously
along country roads, and then, when we arrive
he lifts the latch to the kitchen door.

In the parlour are Tadcu's handwritten books,
all the cows he's ever milked in alphabetical order:
Abertha, Aelwen, Deryn, all letters down to Wynn

and I walk in the fields where the diviner found water,
and the cesspit where Max the spaniel drowned,
and the daisies are begging in the moonlight

not to be trodden down into the earth. One blade of grass
stands to make a field, a thousand daisies a wreath.
Me for once striding over this field wanting

the dark to stay as it covets this silence
and permits the dead to turn in their sleep
and the dying to keep the night with them.

To live in Wales is to be conscious
At dusk of the spilled blood
That went into the making of a wild sky...

R.S.Thomas   Welsh Landscape

Welsh woman

I was born into a family of Welsh women
whose souls have fled to the hills, flown
to their own versions of heaven and hell

or purgatory for whom there will be no more *capel*
on Sundays, no more cameos to be pinned to blouses
for weddings or funerals and no more unbolting

of front doors for special occasions. These old women
have taken to roost in the treetops, caw to one another
as dawn awakens the skies. They praise the changing

seasons and delight in the rustle of feathers and leaves
and petticoats. And they preen while telling their stories
to make each other blush.

The ash grove alone is my home...

even now decades later the words ring in my head
you're singing, laughing, nimble fingers over keys
a sexless uniform that clings to your breasts
national health glasses that need cleaning
and every morning after prefects did room check
I'd go down to the music cells

watch your hands, never take my eyes from you
only one morning we weren't quick enough
and we were found in bed, punished
for being young away from home
but I can't say homesick because you gave me
a friendship that I hadn't known existed

you helped me to read music, pronounce in Welsh
the words you wanted me to learn
but in the end there wasn't time
Ah! Then little thought of how soon we should part
so I only learnt fragments to do with the sea
and on the cliffs at Pendine

whether it's summer or nearly summer
were we ever as young as that, who were we
for the word pervert still smarts
your specs blurred with tears
my stammer on the prefect's words
Amid the dark shades of the lonely ash grove

The doctor's family

I am the eldest daughter. No one watches
as I push potatoes from my plate
into a pocket to flush away later.

My father sits at the head, hands splayed,
nine-inch span, nails manicured
for examining patients.

My mother spoons out Welsh beef casserole.
No one speaks. Twilight falls on five of us.
Evening moves across the kitchen, settles

on cherries on the window sill, darkens the fruit
to be placed on the table after we've eaten –
black shining cherries, faded Formica.

Moscow, January

It's 1974, black-market streets, ice pavements
Even the food didn't warm, hard boiled eggs

floating in cabbage broth. Every bit of the cold
I was responsible for – failed marriage, carrying a child

with a man I thought could have been a husband
– I tried to phone home.

My money didn't understand the system and roubles
dropped through. Every night I prayed to a God

I no longer believed in and tried to imagine Mamgu,
disbelief in her voice, *Fy Dduw, Fy Dduw, bach…*

Fy Dduw: My God
bach: dear, little one

Warsaw '76

The sky is a pause   No beginning
or ending   the grey of it   the paleness
I'd bought daffodils and bread

Back at the flat I'd heat up borscht
and dry tea-bags for re-use
Sharper   colder the stubborn flakes
brought messages which stilled the day

The moment of walking away into Mass
Christ's heart-blood spilled into streets
This was not home
Zimner the old woman said,

pointing to my baby   taking the last of my zloty
to enter the church   I was hoping for a warmer God
You brought me to this city
and left me   taking my English currency

This cold never experienced before
My mind in compartments
one for survival   one for common sense
one for seeking some kind of faith

Zimner: cold

Keshite uchi wasurenai

I'd call and you'd answer in grunts, *huh, uh, um,*
and your step-father would despair at money

wasted on French exchanges.
That was when landlines carried messages

but now, on visits home, you speak to colleagues
from a tiny phone in Japanese, Thai, Vietnamese.

And we have come to places to visit you.
We thought the door was closed on your past

but you left it ajar – on your bedroom walls
are photographs of haystacks, a farmhouse,

you in a rock pool with your brother,
the old oak that overlooks our house and

one of me with you, tiny, in my arms
taken with a polaroid and fading.

Keshite uchi wasurenai: Japanese, I'll never forget home

We'll never know about the fire 2000

i.m. Edith Thomas, step-grandmother

Llawhaden, once the house we'd never dreamt of entering,
almost belonged to us. Llawhaden. The name rolled

off our tongues like cream. We trailed after Edith to hear
her talking to the cows, helped to collect eggs and listened

to her on the Bethesda organ. The house with two staircases
that led up into the eaves, higher than we'd ever been before.

The house where Cromwell stayed. Stories of how he walked at
night.
We believed her every word. His smile. His helmet. Nothing to
doubt.

We count the steps of disappearing, how she crept upstairs to bed
in that old familiar way. Which staircase?

Some say it was a two-bar electric.

Bara Brith

because I'm my mother's daughter
it's important to get the millilitres
of water right for this loaf
to soak the sultanas and sugar
overnight so they absorb the tea

it's 6 o'clock somewhere in the world
my father says, quoting Graham Greene
and pours his whisky, *Tut,* my mother says
thinking of her ancestors and the pot
that is never empty

Elan Valley

The old bench is rollicking on the waves
My father commented as he looked through the window

Summer or winter, rain flooded the shop on the corner
which sold stacked tins of broken biscuits

a toothless woman serving treats, ha'penny chews
On the wall pictures of sailors, sons sunk at sea

Rain turned dusty days and parties to wash-outs
while teenage years rampaged like floods through streets

Then the rain in the Elan Valley believing he'd be here forever
Now driving rain slashes tracks that lead to Pendine sands

Waves hit the shore, the sun and its halo have disappeared
he's gone   he'll always be here

waves carry him back   away and back

The Commiphora Myrrh Tree

Physician, heal thyself
    New Testament: St Luke

for P. H.
First British Heart Foundation Professor of Cardiology

They wound the trees to bleed them of their resin,
pictures demonstrate fact and him, dead.

He, twenty years my senior, so at ease in the world,
why leave it so suddenly?

Did he lose direction from his lab into the mortuary
and then not know how to exit?

Did he die wondering about all he'd pioneered?
Were his heart, paintings, violin, aspirations over-ruled,

voted out as he was left on a cold slab, in a busy hospital,
an unremarkable day for his own autopsy?

And had he watched the bleeding of the trees
to collect resin for this myrrh, his present from Jerusalem?

Grey

I am the Mamgu now.
I love boys with wrinkled socks
that barely cover their ankles.
I eat the smoky-grey jellies first.
I look for grey shapes in the night
and love the stillness of snow,
the fox's prints left on the lawn.

The church stands on its own path

And I, a small Welsh woman, sit in a pew
as I might have done a hundred years ago,
believing in the passing of the seasons

and I wonder what soul would have come
so far from anywhere and felt a need for this
one small orange and green stained-glass window,

a rattling door, yet there is a presence here
as a non-believer I honour –
the dark after the light, today's light fading.

What night knows

I woke the night up   you slept on
although I knew you were there   you were not there

and in the moments that followed   this presence
that had disappeared   re-appeared and beckoned

as retreating waves beckon   the shore
I could no longer tread the path   already forgotten

the swim in the Irish sea   the coldest day of the year
sand stinging   my legs arms face

you stirred   all the untruths came flooding back
slept on   knowing me well   knowing little

The path

I have come here before during a long day
even though the way is difficult
and the path obscured by old tractors

The winter's been harsh, wind-slashing rain
a child's abandoned wellington is awash
with weeds and grease, mice have made nests

The farmhouse still stands, cattle stalls are empty
cow pats recycled by dung beetles
the kitchen garden is overgrown

The mind returns to where it has been
even though the way is difficult
and the path obscured

Wiseman's Bridge

I watch an old man slip on the pebbled beach,
I retrieve his glasses

as once I would have done my father's
and as the old man's vision stays blurred

he smiles into a distance, points in the direction
of a door, paint-peeled from the salt of the sea

I have come to love the fisherman's upturned boat
sea-weed darkened on the shingle

I've forgotten a truth I once knew
the music is there in the ache of my body

We once climbed Snowdon

my father is leading the way fearful
we'd never reach the bottom again
or see the grass veer to the left of the footpath

the sooner we realise there's not much
except the sound of grasses
blown around the mountain oak

the sooner we let sleep drift we allow dreams in
my mother's voice calls throughout the night
Remember to feed your father –

sleep well, her voice comes in and out
and I thought this is how it should be
camping near Snowdon in the old farmer's field

the horse is lame and my father whispers
he is going to die, but I knew he was dead already
sometimes we hear the wind and sometimes a whisper

Photograph

The way the camera's angled, is the gin half empty?
The tonic's gone beside the gnocchi, left-over sausages.

It's hard to see whether there are cherries left on the trees.
Perhaps we've eaten them as they dropped, dark, almost black,

into our hands – you're never in the photographs,
the only one who can hold the camera steady.

Someone's talking but there's laughter as we remembered
the slowworm that slithered through the stillness when we arrived

and you threw the blue cloth over the table to make life respectable
before adding forks and neatly polished glasses.

We're posed like a summer sketch found in an old crimson notebook
and I think blue cloth, cherries, against a backdrop of horses.

Ferries

There was the ferry to Caldey, waves thrashing
over the side of the boat and children laughing,
dogs perturbed. Once on the island we found

thirteen bald monks chanting their morning rituals.
The Abbey stood in splendour and daisies.
Money passed through hands as with money lenders

in the temple but it was spent on cheap tokens
children love, forget, lose by nightfall. This day
disappeared, sounds of chanting, waves hitting the ferry.

And then, not until now, do I think of that ferry
but here a young man sits and the sun beats down
on his bright red bird-of-paradise hair.

He heads with the rest of us to Hampton Court.
But this is the sort of time, dad, you come back,
roses in the vase by your bed, roses the flowers

you knew, your blue eyes, blind, searching,
as you ask questions, wanting to connect meaning,
however thinly, with the taut band of belonging.

It's only now I begin to know you, how you would turn
to look for us when walking,
how you would look into our faces.

Two sons

long overcoats
collars pulled up to their ears
walk – walk –
down to the retreating waves

sand sucks their footprints
no one would know where their steps had trod
it was you might say a perfect ending
for when does an evening end

and a walk to the sea begin
hermit crabs may have been disturbed
bladder-wrack swept to shore-lines
I wish the sands would care

Minnows

Once I thought I knew what it was,
this thing flying through the air

or moving like a minnow through water,
delicate and hard to fathom but there.
Definitely there.

Once my boys tried to catch minnows
and then released them back to the river.
Did they suddenly understand, have
knowledge of this thing that hovers above me?
Did they know I would preserve this moment?

If I stretch my arm as far as it will go
and look at my elongated fingers
I can hear a breath like a man's laughter
as he confesses to playing the wrong notes,
but they were notes. That melody over the waves.

It was there and this thing I thought I once knew
is there still out of reach and nearer the sky
than I like. A net flying might catch it,

so quick and gone. I can almost decipher its colour,
silver and minnow-like and silver.

Swimming

i.m.Rachael

Rebecca, Ben, Tom, Raph in swimming costumes
are about to jump into the river – the river that separates

the fields near the old house, ignoring the water rat
who owns this river, everyone to jump except you,

standing in that shabby coat you always wore,
holding the towels for the wet shivering bodies

when they return. Your head leans to one side
always when listening intently but now it's me

holding the towels and you can dive into the waters too
swim the width and leap up to catch the ball

hair glistening in the wet, the sun highlights
that emerald costume bought for sunny days.

From the other side of the hedge the cows are heard.
It's 3am and I can't sleep, waiting for time to curve

to leap back on itself so I can wave from the river bank
and you can give me the thumbs up, back.

Ar Hyd y Nos
All through the night

through the night the sea hits the shore
through the night it calls your names
the waves say your names
just answer yes
any of you just answer yes

One Day

At our father's funeral you played Bach, so gentle
Now the world, as it is, you can't pick up
your instrument and join in with other musicians.

There's a score of a song on the walls of your new house
and I hear the first notes to be played on your saxophone
which, for the moment, lies idle in the corner of a room.

It doesn't suit you not to play and make people happy.

You will have plenty of music in your house!
Your children are creating assault courses,
jungles, over and around old furniture, the settee

you once wanted to abandon, but plans seldom work.
Rebecca goes each day to the front line
and you worry. The children will need lunch

but outside there will be the smell of the lilac,
the garlic and the fox will slink across your lawn at night.
All of these things are music and we wait until we hear you.

And we will, again and again and again.

Full of Covid 19

For Ewan on the Isle of Skye

The picture in the newspaper takes me to hills
where you're helping your parents with lambing
but you'd rather be with your new wife in the heat

and busyness of tuk-tuks, the frenzied way of Bangkok,
finishing your PhD, deciding on a future far from here.
Your parents too elderly to fly over mountains and oceans –

you travelled to them, the long, cold nights you had left.
And over the road from our house Clare sews gowns
for the most at risk in the front-line. Protective clothing

from Turkey held up on route. One particle is capable
of destroying lives. Meanwhile in the road children are
happy on bikes, one family at a time, out to play.

And your video has clicked in – the sea in the distance,
twin lambs just born, licked clean by their mother
and you are content to be as one, there, for now.